TOTALLY
TULIPS

TOTALLY TULIPS

by

Matt Damsker

Illustrated by
Carolyn Vibbert

CELESTIAL ARTS
BERKELEY, CALIFORNIA

To the flowers in my garden:
Lori, Jesse, Ashley, and Sugar

Celestial Arts Publishing
P.O. Box 7123
Berkeley, CA 94707

Cover design and illustration: Bob Greisen
Interior design and typesetting: Susan Hernday
Interior illustrations: Carolyn Vibbert

Totally Tulips is produced by becker&mayer!, Ltd.
Printed in Singapore
ISBN 0-89087-780-7

Library of Congress Catalog Card Number: 95-71815

First Printing, 1996

1 2 3 4 / 99 98 97 96

Other books in the Totally Flowers series:
Totally Orchids
Totally Roses
Totally Sunflowers

Not one of Flora's brilliant race
A form more perfect can display;
Art could not feign more simple grace
Nor nature take a line away.
　　　—*James Montgomery*

TABLE OF CONTENTS

TOTALLY
TULIPS

THE JOY OF
TULIPS

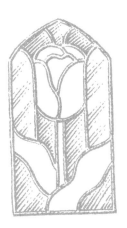

Does anything announce springtime so boldly as a proud stand of tall tulips? Wavering in the breeze yet firmly at attention, tulips are the garden's colorful sentinels—perennial, reliable, trembling with all the promise of summer. The glory of tulips is utterly sensual; their deep hues kiss the eye, their velvety petals delight the touch, but the joy of tulips has more to do with the ease of sowing their delicate bulbs, and seeing them, year upon year, in sizes, shapes, and colors to suit any taste.

Tulips are ideal for spring borders or beds, affording vividness and height, and adding structure to informal mixings that may include daffodils or other spring flowers. The simple strategy of planting early, mid-, and late flowering tulips assures a sequence of blooms that can make even the neophyte gardener feel wizardly. And yes, they can be grown virtually anywhere (outside of the hottest of the hot climes), thriving in sunny or sheltered sites, asking only for some fertile, well-drained soil. Many varieties are true perennials and will flourish yearly; others are more short-lived, and are best removed after a few years.

Horticulturists have divided tulips into fifteen categories by appearance and seasonality, but as a grower you don't have to get so technical. Basically, you'll be choosing from hybrid and/or species tulips, and by their bloom times (early, mid-, or late season).

TULIP TYPES

Hybrid tulips are the popular standards—
bred for centuries and combining the most
desirable traits of the original types. The
tall-stemmed (eighteen inches or more),
classically cupped blooms of the popular
Darwin hybrids, in flaming reds and yellows, typify tulips to most people. But
hybrids are widely varied as well, growing
in delicate lily shapes, with fringed petals,
with doubled, peony-like blooms, and in
swirling, painterly color mixes that earn
them the sobriquet of Rembrandt hybrids.

As for species tulips, these are mostly
hybrids that retain the characteristics of
the originals—the primary tulip "species"
that gave rise to their mixed-breed cousins.
Species tulips are typically small, rarely

taller than six or eight inches, and tend to be the earliest bloomers. Their flowers often last longer than later bloomers, because they are preserved by the cool early spring weather.

It won't take you long to calculate a tulip bloom schedule like a pro if you start with a stand of lovely species types that will bloom with the daffodils, followed by early hybrids that bloom when the daffodils fade, with a few mid- and late season choices to follow. Of course, the appeal of tulips has a lot to do with how easy they are to grow, but the more you learn about them, the more they have to offer to your garden.

Exotic Origins

Tulips are taken for granted these days, but unlike other staples of the flower garden, their history is one of exotic origin and even intrigue. A tulip is an herb; it's also any of about 150 spring-flowering bulbs in the genus *Tulipa*, of the Lilaceae (Lily) family. They are native to Asia and the Mediterranean area, where wild tulips are small and lily-like.

After centuries of hybridization, the roots of today's garden tulips are hard to trace, but a cultivated form of the bulb first appeared in western Europe during the sixteenth century, via the trade routes that led to Constantinople and the west.

An Austrian diplomat, Ogier Ghiselin de Busbecque, is credited with bringing tulip seeds and bulbs to his Vienna garden from his travels in the Turkish empire. Indeed, Busbecque's journals from 1554 contain the first European reference to the tulip.

The Dutch botanist Carolus Clusius acquired the first tulips in Holland from Busbecque; one account has it that Clusius hoarded them until they were stolen by a wily entrepreneur who distributed them at great profit. The flowers were increasingly prized as specimens of Oriental mystery and perfection. One English diarist of the late 1500s, intoxicated by the sight of tulips in bloom at a Mediterranean port, celebrated the "lyssomey and scarleted goblet, the tulipams, as one would be proffered a small draught of nectar…."

Flower of a Romeo

Few flowers are more associated with Eros than the tulip, and it's a reputation rooted in the earliest days of the bulb's cultivation. One legend (which may even be a partial source for Shakespeare's *Romeo and Juliet*) has it that a Persian youth named Farad was desperately enamored of a maiden named Shirin. One day, Farad received false news of Shirin's death. Blind with grief, he mounted his horse and galloped over a cliff to his death. The blood from his many wounds stained the earth, and from each stain, the legend goes, a scarlet tulip sprang.

FEVERISH DEMAND

Indeed, no other flower in history seems to have sparked a cultural craze, but that's exactly what happened in the Netherlands, a land now synonymous with flower bulbs. By 1634, the demand for tulips had risen to such a feverish pitch that enormous prices—equal to thousands of dollars in today's market—were being paid for single bulbs. During this "tulipomania," as it came to be called, fortunes rose and fell amid rampant speculation in tulip stock. The Dutch government eventually had to regulate the tulip trade after countless bankruptcies had been provoked by tulip profiteers.

By then the Dutch had all but cornered the tulip industry, and the Netherlands' dominance in today's flower bulb market is an outgrowth of the tulipomania era. All the same, tulip growers around Europe and in North America have been producing worthy generations of hybrid beauties, leading to a world market for tulips that's a boon to any gardener, with a wide variety of high-quality bulbs available at affordable prices.

One bulb of a red-and-white tulip known as SEMPER AUGUSTUS *sold at a seventeenth century European auction for what would be today's equivalent of $1,200. The following year two bulbs propagated from that first one sold for $30,000.*

THE BEST
OF THE BULBS

Ask a hundred tulip fanciers which type they favor, and you'll likely get a hundred different replies. Tulipomania is intensely personal, after all. Those who feel passionately for the tall, bulbous blooms of the classic hybrids are apt to turn a nose up at the subtler, faux-lily look of tiny species tulips, and vice versa. Mixing types and bloom times is the best way not only to gauge your passion for certain tulips, but to judge the best choices for your area. Here's a primer of tulip varieties that have proven the most enduringly popular—as much for their reliability as for their good looks.

DARWIN HYBRIDS

Big blooms and tall, sturdy stems
make Darwin hybrids prime choices for
no-nonsense tulip growing. Blooming
mid-season, from about late April through
early May, they make a showy stand, as
high as thirty inches, with larger flowers
than any other tulip type. Best of all, they
come in a dizzying variety of rich colors
(some are bicolored), so there's really no
need to view Darwins, however typical
they may be in terms of tulip style, as
run-of-the-mill choices. OXFORD is a
ravishing red-orange variety, while
GUDOSHNIK is a heart-stopping yellow
streaked with red. The pure yellow of
SWEET HARMONY or the pristine white of

MAUREEN are calming influences, while JEWEL OF SPRING is a playful pale yellow edged with crimson.

The Darwin tulip, named for Charles Darwin, was bred in the late nineteenth century by Dutch growers. In 1892, the Darwin won the only horticultural gold medal at the Paris International Exhibition.

REMBRANDTS

These were the most precious bulbs of Europe's tulipomania era of the seventeenth century, and no wonder. The bicolored petals seem finely painted, as if by the Dutch master's hand. Rembrandts are "broken" tulips—that is, striped or spotted. This occurs as a result of a pigmentation that's been traced to a flower virus, and is manipulated through breeding. These masterworks blend violet, apricot, reds, yellows, and whites in unforgettable lyric swirls, and can reach two feet high.

"Clean as a lady, cool as glass, fresh without fragrance the tulip was."

—HUMBERT WOLFE

LILY-FLOWERED

It takes a slightly better trained eye to recognize these delicacies as tulips. Their blooms are thinner and more pointed—indeed, more lily-like—than the classic hybrids, but they are classics on their own terms. The bulbs bloom in mid-season, about early May, on stems up to two feet high. The fierce hues of ALADDIN and RED SHINE balance delicacy with intensity, while WHITE TRIUMPHATOR is so blanc de blanc it almost seems lit from within.

BEST OF THE LILY TYPES

Tulip connoisseurs often cherish the pointed-petal delicacy of the lily-flowering varieties. A beguiling mix of some of the best lily-flowered types would include: ALADDIN, with its deep, yellow-edged red; BALLADE, bright violet with white edging; CHINA PINK; ELEGANT LADY, a yellow edged in red-violet; pale pink JACQUELINE; white-edged, violet MAYTIME; and yellow-edged, sinfully red QUEEN OF SHEBA.

"...An abundance of flowers everywhere—narcissus, hyacinths, and those which the Turks call tulipam—much to our astonishment, because it was almost mid-winter, a season unfriendly to flowers."

—OGIER GHISELIN DE BUSBECQUE

SINGLE EARLIES

Blooming during the first half of April in most areas, single early tulips are available in countless colors and blends. They're a great choice for kick-starting your spring fever, with sturdy, twelve-inch stems. PRINCESS IRENE is a dramatic choice, blending salmon and red tones to remarkable effect, along with the intense red of COULEUR CARDINAL, and the yellow-edged red KEIZERSKROON. Single earlies typically bloom long into the cool days of April, and many will rebloom for as many as nine or ten years.

DOUBLE EARLIES/DOUBLE LATES

These gems extend the typical cupped tulip look with a large "doubled" or multiple bloom, which is a frillier, more peony-like profusion of petals per flower. They also bloom in the first half of April, on eight- to twelve-inch stems. MONTE CARLO is a sunburst of yellow that tulip fanciers often rave about, while the rosy PEACH BLOSSOM is a can't-miss favorite. And while we're on double earlies, be apprised that there are also double lates—they've got the same characteristics as their April-blooming brethren, but bloom instead from mid- to late May in most areas, growing an inch or so taller.

COTTAGE TULIPS

These delights have a tightly compacted egg shape, but grow impressively tall—up to thirty inches. They're named for the English cottage gardens in which they were discovered, and they're usually the latest-blooming tulips of the spring. If there's a secret to taking advantage of this type, it's to plant them in quantity. Not only will they look spectacular in great graceful, wavering masses, but in the process they cover the browned leaves of the earlier-blooming tulips you had behind them.

PARROT TULIPS

Showy and special, parrot tulips sport birdlike plumage—ruffled, twisted, or fringed petals in any number of colors and swirls. They grow to about twenty inches on especially firm stalks, and most are late bloomers that do as well in shade as in sun. If you're looking for parroty drama, BLACK PARROT offers the deepest of purples—a show-stopper against white or yellow tulips—while the widely popular ESTELLA RIJNVELD features a red-and-white pinwheel pattern. But you can find subtler apricot, lilac, and pink-hued flowers as well.

FRINGED TULIPS

There are fringed parrot tulips, of course,
but the unique, lacy quality of fringing—
in which the petals are serrated along their
points or along their entire lengths—
makes fringed tulips a type unto themselves. Most are mid-season flowers,
blooming around early May, and reach
fifteen to twenty-four inches in height.
BLUE HERON, like all flowers with the word
"blue" in their names, is actually a variant
of purple, but with a red tone that adds
wine-like complexity to the fringy display.
BURGUNDY LACE is another popular choice
in fringe.

T. FOSTERIANA

The "*T.*" before the *fosteriana* indicates that these are species tulips, and indeed, these showy delights are virtually the same today as in their wild state centuries ago on the Asian steppes. True to most species tulips, they bloom early in April and get about sixteen inches tall. Color choices are many, with a variety of intense hues and large blooms. *Fosterianas* are, as one expects of species tulips, hardy and reliably perennial.

When buying bulbs, be sure they're firm and undamaged, with well-defined growing points. If you note any soft areas at all, reject them.

T. Greigii

Greigii are dainty and versatile, growing no higher than about ten inches, but with lovely, variegated foliage striped with purples and reds—which makes them almost as desirable as a bedding or border planting, blooms or not. However, the blooms are showy and long-wearing, in drop-dead crimsons, golds, salmons and mixes of red, yellow, and white. Plaisir is a two-toned pleaser, while Red Riding Hood—such big red petals it has! *Greigii* bloom from mid-April to early May.

T. KAUFMANNIANA

Also called the waterlily tulip, this species treasure has open-spreading, pointed petals, and is usually the first tulip to bloom, late in March or at the beginning of April. Many choices also have striped or spotted foliage. Growing not much higher than six inches with spreading blooms, they're superb for rock gardens or massed in broad flower beds. The pale salmon of FRITZ KREISLER—named for the great violinist, who may or may not have been as great a tulipomaniac—has made it a tulip of choice for decades.

TOP PERFORMERS

If you want to be sure your tulip plantings will yield reliably year after year, purchase bulbs labeled "good" for naturalizing or perennializing. Catalogs usually point this out quite clearly; you may have to ask an expert at your garden center for more information on unlabeled bulbs. But experts agree that hybrid tulips are your best bet for performance. Among single early tulips, try KEIZERKROON, CHRISTMAS MARVEL, and COULEUR CARDINAL. Among fringed tulips, look for BURGUNDY LACE. And you'll rarely go wrong with any of the Darwin hybrids in any of their solid or two-toned shades.

Newest of the New

The nature of flower breeding means that a "new" tulip can take from 15 to 25 years to come to market. That's because years of trial and error—crossing strains and charting progress over several seasons before concluding that a new hybrid is worth pursuing—are followed by more years required for a grower to build up commercial stocks of the new variety. Here's a rundown of some of the most highly touted new varieties out of the Netherlands:

DR. AN WANG: This single early is a unique shade of lilac blue, and grows up to a tall fifteen inches.

Fancy Frills: a fringed variety, with a rose-pink blossom and flames of creamy white. Long-lasting blooms.

Pink Impression: large, egg-shaped Darwin hybrid blossoms with deep rose petals in blurred, dreamy shades. The long-lasting flowers grow on thiry-inch stems.

Marilyn: a lily-flowered charmer with fuchsia-red stripes on shocking white.

Spring Green: creamy white and feathered with a soft green. Late-blooming. The upward ruffling is classic of the green Viridifloras.

Praestans Unicum: This unique species tulip looks like a yellow-bordered, wide-leafed hosta (plantain lily), with up to five red blooms per stem.

HAPPY FAMILY: late-season, and multi-flowering, with three to five fuchsia flowers per bulb.

DREAMLAND: soft white and deep blushing red on the outside, rosy shades inside the cup. Single late.

"Rough winds do shake the darling buds of May."
—SHAKESPEARE

CULTIVATION, CARE &
TULIP TECHNIQUE

When to Plant

Spring-blooming flowers need fall planting, and tulips need a few weeks to set their roots before the deep freeze of winter. If the bulb freezes before rooting, it's a goner. So plant in cool, mid-fall weather to avoid a reversion to unseasonable warmth which might cause the bulbs to "spring" prematurely. But even if you're late in planting, you can still sow with confidence so long as the ground isn't frozen—and you'll find that the soil is pretty forgiving on that count in most areas, since it takes a lot of extended frigidity to freeze the top foot or so of soil.

Tulips must have cold weather to bloom year after year, so if you live in hot zones (USDA zone eight or nine), you'll probably be treating them as annual flowers, blooming only once. But that doesn't mean you can't do a fall planting of tulips for a spring bloom even if your climate never gets cold enough to chill the bulbs as they require. So the secret is to chill the bulbs before they go in the ground! Just store them in a paper bag in the refrigerator for about eight weeks before you plant and they'll be fine for fall.

"Anyone who has a bulb has spring. Bulbs don't need much light; they don't need good soil; and they don't need cosseting. They are, in fact, the horticultural equivalent of cats...."
—ANONYMOUS

DOES SIZE MATTER?

At auction in the Netherlands bulbs are sold by their circumference size (called the "caliber"). The bigger the bulb, the bigger the flower it will yield; typically, larger-caliber bulbs fetch a higher price. But don't conclude that bigger is always better. For your showiest planting sites, yes, it makes sense to invest in the largest bulbs. But smaller-caliber bulbs are a more economical way to add color to large, or marginal, areas.

"June brings tulips, lilies, roses,
Fills the children's hands with posies."
—SARA COLERIDGE

TULIP PLANTING TIMES FOR
NORTH AMERICA

UNITED STATES:

New England/northern states:	Sept.–Nov.
Mid-Atlantic states:	Oct.–Nov.
Rocky Mt. states:	Oct.–Nov.
Northwest:	Oct.–Nov.
South and Gulf Coast states:	Oct.–Jan.
Southern Cal. and Southwest:	Oct.–Dec.

CANADA:

British Columbia:	Oct.–Nov.
Prairie provinces:	Sept.
Eastern provinces:	Sept.–Oct.

Making the Bed

Be sure your planting areas are healthy and smoothly raked before planting tulips. The soil should be loose and well-drained, since waterlogged bulbs will only rot. If the soil is tight and soggy, till it or spade it up and add enough compost or other organic material to loosen the soil and aid the drainage. Be sure the area gets at least partial sun.

Plant dry bulbs as soon as possible after you purchase them. If your bulbs have been stored over the winter, plant them as soon as possible in spring, before they start putting out shoots. Bulbs grown in pots can be planted anytime during the growing season, or kept potted until they die down, then replanted in fall as dry bulbs.

Preparing the Hole

You can use a trowel or specially designed bulb planter to sow your tulips, and with a little preparation, you will achieve great results. No matter how fertile your soil may be, a small handful of bonemeal added to the bottom of each bulb hole is a good idea. Be sure you place the bulb with its broad end down (or it'll be hopelessly upside down). As for planting depth and bulb spacing, they vary somewhat with tulip type, but most of them will do fine at eight inches deep and six inches apart. In fact, unless your bulb supplier tells you a specific depth and spacing, "eight by six" is a comfy rule of thumb.

FERTILE ADVICE

Fall and spring fertilization of your bulbs is the rule. But if you intend to treat your tulips as once-and-done annuals—as many gardeners do, preferring to start fresh each year with new colors and types—then no fertilizer is necessary. That's because healthy bulbs have plenty of nourishment stored up to assure blooms the first season. If perennial performance is your wish, low-nitrogen fertilizer such as well-rotted cow manure is an easy choice for fall; in spring, a high-nitrogen, quick-release fertilizer will enhance future flowerings.

"The Amen! of Nature is always a flower."
—OLIVER WENDELL HOLMES

SPECIAL EFFECTS

Obviously, where you place your bulbs will have the most profound impact on where the blooms appear above ground, so you want to give some thought to that. Tulips that return perennially will divide over the years, and pop up wonderfully in unexpected spots, but in general, what you sow is what you get. Bulbs planted closer together than the typical six inches (and the smaller the bulbs, the closer together you can place them) will appear in bunches, which has more impact than planting them in precise (read "boring") rows; or you can plant them in triangular or circular patterns to get interesting geometric effects.

The Natural Look

A favorite approach to planting tulips is to "naturalize" them. All this means is you're strewing them more or less at random so that the flowers will appear as if they popped up naturally in an unspoiled meadow. You can naturalize in a flower bed, or under a tree, or anywhere you want the natural look. Just take handfuls of bulbs and toss them gently around the planting site. Then dig the holes wherever the bulbs land and plant them. Don't worry about spacing, since some will be bunched and others far apart—that's the carefree beauty of the effect.

CRITTER CONTROL

Rodents, rabbits, deer, and other furry fiends love to munch on the sweet, onion-like layers of flower bulbs, and tulips are especially attractive to them. Although the critters will rarely bother the foliage, stalks, and blooms of the flower itself, they'll dig through your loose soil with ease to get to the bulbs. If this is a problem in your area, an easy and proven solution is to plant the bulbs in a wire cage or cages, depending on how many bulbs you have. Set the cages at the proper planting depth in the ground, place bulbs on the cage bottoms, and fill with soil. The roots will grow right through the wire, but the critters will be hard put to penetrate it. Another technique is to sprinkle some dried bloodmeal on the shoots when they emerge in spring, and on and around the foliage later in the season; most critters hate the smell and will avoid the beds.

"If a change in a tulip is effected, one goes to a florist and tells him, and soon it gets talked about. Everyone is anxious to see it. If it is a new flower, each one gives an opinion... If it looks like an Admiral you call it General or any other name you fancy, and send a bottle of wine to your friends that they may remember to talk about it."

—A SEVENTEENTH CENTURY DUTCH AUTHOR,
AT THE TIME OF TULIPOMANIA

FOOD AND WATER

Feeding your bulbs the right fertilizer just after planting and regularly after that can help assure hardy blooms for years. Use a fertilizer with a 5-10-12 ratio (that's five parts nitrogen, ten parts phosphorus, and twelve parts potassium) and feed the plants each fall at about the same time as when you originally planted them, and again about a month and a half prior to bloom time. As for watering your bulbs, in most moderate climates you won't need to do much watering after the bulbs have established themselves. After planting, water the bulbs weekly until the ground hardens; come spring, all they'll need is a weekly watering—but only if there's no spring rain. Don't water at all during the summer.

TEMPERATURE SWINGS

In many areas, early spring temperatures can swing drastically, affecting the sprouting habits of your tulips. But healthy bulbs will usually withstand the most extreme cold, snow, or even early hot spells, according to experts at the International Flower Bulb Center in Holland. So when a sudden spring freeze hits, there's no real need to cover your sprouting tulips with blanketing or mulch, despite what your neighbors may advise. The worst that can happen is a few open blossoms may become slightly "freezer burnt." Unseasonable warmth in late winter may cause early sprouting and blooming of some bulbs, but this won't damage their blooming capacity in subsequent years.

DIVIDING CROWDED TULIP BULBS

If your mature tulips seem to flower less than in previous years, the problem is usually a matter of overcrowding. This is easy to correct, but requires some careful doctoring. First, use a garden fork to lift the entire bulb clump from the ground. Do this as the foliage is dying, and take care not to damage the bulbs. Next, divide the clumps of bulbs by hand, first into smaller clumps and then into individual bulbs. Remove any dead or diseased matter. Finally, clean the bulbs, removing their loose coats or "tunics," and replant in freshly readied soil.

PROPAGATING TULIPS FROM OFFSETS

Tulips increase their numbers naturally by producing offsets around the bulb, and you can propagate these babies by separating them from their parent bulbs. Wait until spring, before any active growth begins, and lift a clump of bulbs carefully with a garden fork. Shake off any excess soil and separate the clumps by hand. Then find a large bulb with several well-developed offsets; clean the soil off these and pull them gently away from the parent bulb, preserving any roots. Replant the parent bulbs in your garden, and pot the offsets—one per pot—in six-inch clay or plastic pots. Place the offsets in a moist, sandy soil mixture, cover it with an inch or so of soil, and water. Let them grow for one or two seasons in a cool spot indoors with indirect light, then plant in your garden in fall.

A new variety of tulip results when cultivated varieties "break," or mutate, yielding new colors and color patterns. More recently, scientists have learned that breaks are a combination of genetic mutation and a tulip virus. The swirled Rembrandt tulips are a classic example of this.

Foliage Do's and Don'ts

Once the beauteous blooms are gone, you'll be left with deflowered tulip stalks—and a mighty temptation to trim away the stems and clean all those scraggly, strap-like tulip leaves off the ground. *But that's the last thing you should do.* The foliage is actually feeding the buried bulb precious energy from the sunlight, without which it won't be as hardy the following year. Let the foliage lie until it turns mostly brown and crisp, at which point you can snip off the stem below the leaves at ground level. The best way to hide the browning leaves without discarding or folding them is to make sure you've planted late-flowering tulips and other summer flowers that will somewhat camouflage the old foliage.

SHOWY BLEND
SUGGESTIONS

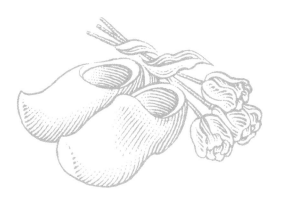

In Raised Planters

Tulips are glorious in any ground setting, but can be even more glorious off the ground. A long, raised wooden planter will provide excellent drainage and a great proscenium for the right tulips. Try a blend of APRICOT BEAUTY, with its pastel tone, and the tall, purple SCOTCH LASSIE or pink ROSEWORTHY. This blend of contrasting height and complementing color is at the heart of good tulip design. And remember, in planters or in any ground site, plant masses of bulbs—not straight rows, which will yield a thin, uninteresting effect.

YELLOWS AND REDS

Reds and yellows are certainly the most vivid—and the most popular—blend of tulip color, but the secret to getting it right is to blend the right tulips and avoid mere ostentation. The tall Darwin hybrids are often the best choices for an early-season burst of color. Mixing QUEEN WILHELMINA, with its blush of red-in-yellow, with the bold crimson of OXFORD or GENERAL EISENHOWER is a surefire strategy. For mid-season, red-yellow BING CROSBY blushes deeply and well against the bicolored beauty of GOLDEN MIRJORAN.

The Orange Jewel

Orange is a tough color to use well, but there are so many gorgeous orange-toned tulips that it would be a shame to avoid them. A sure strategy for orangey success? Take the pale coral complexity of APRICOT BEAUTY and intermix it with the delicate petals and fiery orange of *T. fosteriana* ORANGE EMPEROR. Or try the soft orange single early GENERAL DE WET against the pristine white of SNOWSTAR or PAX.

QUEST FOR THE BLACK

The tulip took root in its adopted home-
land of Holland just about 400 years ago,
and from the very beginning the Dutch
breeders were inspired to push the enve-
lope of tulip color. For centuries, hybridiz-
ers have sought the ultimate expression of
tulip majesty and mystery—the black
tulip. Some breeders have drawn close to
the obsidian ideal, but modern experts
conclude that a truly black tulip is an
impossibility. Deep, deep purples like
BLACK PARROT or NEGRITA are about as close
to black as tulips come.

PASTEL PASSION

The bold reds and yellows of many popular tulips make for striking displays, but if you seek a softer, more romanticized look, pastels are the way to go—especially the lavenders, soft pinks, and orange shades. APRICOT BEAUTY and ANGELIQUE happen to be among the most popular in the U.S., and are primary choices for the pastel garden. ANGELIQUE is pink at its palest—semi-double, often looking more like a rose or peony than a tulip. Its flowers are long-lasting in the garden or the vase. APRICOT BEAUTY has a classic goblet shape, but its salmon-rose color, with splashes of fading gold at the edges and a pale green center, may spoil you for any other orange-toned selection. It also blooms earlier than most tulips.

Then there's BLUSHING BEAUTY, thirty inches tall and rosy yellow; a perfect companion for any other pastel. DREAMING MAID is rosy lavender and edged in white. And DOUGLAS BAADER is a pink of remarkable delicacy, almost deceptively white until the light strikes it to reveal the complexity of its tones.

"See how the flowers, as at parade,
Under their colours stand display'd:
Each regiment in order grows,
That of the tulip, pink, and, rose."
—ANDREW MARVELL

LUSTROUS AND LILY-FLOWERED

Lily-flowered tulips are so delicate and distinctive it's hard to go wrong with any blending of them. The driven snow of WHITE TRIUMPHATOR is the perfect foil for rosy MARIETTE lily-flowered tulips, or the bolder ALADDIN or RED SHINE.

TULIPS WITH OTHER BULBS

Tulips become even more versatile when combined with other bulbs. One superb technique for an early awakening of spring color is to mix a deep-hued *T. greigii* such as RED RIDING HOOD with white crocuses, white anemone, or yellow daffodils.

Or mix the pale blue tinge of late-blooming GANDER'S RHAPSODY with pastel hyacinths, or any peony-flowered double-late tulip with soft-hued forget-me-nots or astilbes. And lily-flowered tulips of any hue work well against dark-hued azalea.

As for brightening up drab spots in your landscape, mixing bright reds and deep purples makes for dramatic accenting. Try the intense crimson of single-early COULEUR CARDINAL amid purple pansies or blue hyacinths, or a planting of blue muscari interspersed with OXFORD, which also goes smashingly with Virginia bluebells.

Purple and yellow add familiar beauty at Easter time. A planting of SWEET HARMONY or MONTE CARLO will yield stunning sunbursts against a dainty field of purple crocus.

When arranging cut tulips in bunches, avoid uniformity of size or style—or the result will be a bore. Mix a handful of tall, sturdy, classic Darwin tulips with delicate lily-flowered types and shorter fringed tulips. Go for quality of arrangement, not quantity of blooms.

PLANTING UNDER COVER

Can tulips be planted under ivy or other dense ground covers? Absolutely. They'll grow up through the ground covers quite easily because the tulips begin to sprout well before the leaves of the ground covers have gotten too full to block sunlight. Similarly, tulips planted under trees or deciduous shrubs will sprout with ease, because the bare tree and shrub branches of early spring let plenty of warming sunlight through.

ENJOYING TULIPS
INDOORS

CHOOSING BLOOMS

Tulips are as wonderfully showy inside the home as outside, but snip smartly and they'll last longer indoors. Choose blooms that are neither tightly budded nor fully opened—the ones that are just starting to spread apart are usually best. And be sure to cut the stems with a sharp knife or shears, leaving plenty of foliage on the plants to help them store energy for next season's show.

"Spring comes: The flowers learn their colored shapes."

—MARIA KONOPNICKA

Cutting-and-Keeping Tips

Very late afternoon is the best time to cut tulips, or else in early morning—but bulbs cut during the hot hours of the day tend to fade quickly indoors. Once you've cut the tulips, plunge the stems in a deep vase or container filled with warm water—but no more than 100 degrees F—and place in a cool spot overnight. The next day, place them in a container, change the water, and cut a little of the stem off each day— this exposes fresh stem area that more easily absorbs water. They'll last longest if you keep them cool, and out of direct sun.

Prepping Secrets

A key to keeping your cut tulips colorful for a week or longer is to prepare them properly. A little extra effort goes a long way toward more beautiful and longer-lived floral arrangements. Start by trimming off the white end of the tulip stem with a clean, sharp knife or shears. This opens water intake channels which close when the stem is dry. Next, wrap the tulip bunch snugly in paper or newspaper, leaving the cut lower stems exposed. Position the wrapped bunch upright in a container of cool to lukewarm water just deep enough to cover the exposed stem bases, but not touching the paper. Place the container in a cool spot for an hour or two.

This will help the stems to suction up the water and stiffen in an attractive, upright position.

---

*"Now I am living on Abingdon Square—not the
   Ritz exactly, but a place,*
And I have planted tulips in my windowbox.
*Please God make them come up, so that everyone
   who passes by*
*Will know I'm there, at least long enough to catch
   my breath,*
*When they see the bright, red, beautiful flowers in
   my window."*

—EDWARD FIELD

MIXING TULIPS AND DAFFODILS

Tulips mix especially well with daffodils in cut flower arrangements, but it's important to prepare the daffodils for the vase separately from the tulips, as daffodil stems release a sap-like substance that can harm other flowers. Prepare the daffodils as you would the tulips (see "Prepping Secrets," page 71), but in separate prepping water, which you should discard. Finally, add the daffodils to the tulips in a vase and don't recut the daffodils' stems.

VASE TIPS

Freshly cut tulips will continue to grow as much as an inch in water, so choose your vase accordingly. Darwin hybrid tulips are likely to grow even longer. They'll also provide the longest indoor color. You can maximize the length of your indoor display by removing your tulips from the vase after a week or so, rearranging the still-fresh flowers in a second, smaller vase, and discarding any faded beauties.

"Flowers the blossom!—loaded, swaying arms
Of sated stalks, heaped with pink and white
Of fresh youth's cheek; they lightly throw their charms
Into the fragrance of the deep, wet grass."
                                    —PHILIP LARKIN

LONG-LASTING BLOOMS

Not surprisingly, the big, well-bred Darwin hybrids tend to last a long time indoors— you can't go wrong with cut bunches of red OXFORD or yellow SWEET HARMONY. Personal preference rules in these matters, but a blend of snow-white MAUREEN, pale yellow JEWEL OF SPRING, and just a few splashes of red, via OXFORD or a similar variety, makes for a demure yet dramatic indoor show. Parrot tulips will also endure the indoors quite nicely; a blend of deep purple BLACK PARROT with any of a number of lilac blooms makes for a richly exotic effect. The rosy pastel pink and velvety petals of CLARA BUTT are especially congenial indoors—and long-lasting as well. Experiment at will!

SECRETS OF FORCING

You can enjoy tulips indoors long before they bloom outdoors, of course; the secret is to cause them to bloom, or "force" them. Forcing is easy if you do it right, especially if you choose the right tulips. For starters, choose the right container—clay or plastic pots with drainage holes at the bottom are recommended; just make sure the pot is about twice as deep as your bulbs are long (a three-inch bulb from top to bottom needs a six-inch pot, and so on).

- The potting mixture can be anything recommended for seed-starting. Your garden center can guide you on that, but if you want to make your own soil, combine one-third sphagnum peat moss with one-third sand and one-third store-bought potting soil, and add a cup of perlite or vermiculite per quart. Now you're ready to plant.

- Use pebbles, marbles, or bits of broken flowerpots to cover the drain holes in the pot bottoms, then fill pots about two-thirds full with your soil mixture. Set your bulbs about a half inch below the pot rim, with the flat sides of the bulbs facing the outside of the pot (the first tulip leaves grow from the flat side). Make sure bulbs don't touch each other, then fill the pot with soil, keeping it all loosely packed.

- Water thoroughly, filling with soil as needed.

- Now you've got to chill your potted bulbs, and the easiest ways to do that are either to place them in a refrigerator (never a freezer!) or move them to a cellar or unheated garage and make sure the temperature remains well between 30 and 48 degrees F; also, cover with opaque paper so no light hits the bulbs. Check regularly, and don't let the soil dry out, watering every few weeks.
- After twelve to fourteen weeks of chill, move them to a cool spot (around 58 degrees F) in bright but indirect lighting for about two weeks. Then move them to full sunlight (keep the temperature about the same) for another two weeks. When the buds start to show their colors, get them back to bright, indirect

light but a warmer temperature (about 65 degrees F). Your bulbs will flower for a good long time if you do all this with care. However, tulips won't bloom again after they've been forced, so you can toss them when their petals are spent.

"The Turkish word for tulip is lale *[but an intepreter for Ogier de Busbecque, the Austrian diplomat who introduced the bulb to Europe] probably described the flower as looking like a* thoulypen, *the Turkish word for turban. De Busbecque probably heard 'tulipam,' which ultimately was shortened to 'tulip.'"*

—THEODORE JAMES, JR.
FLOWERING BULBS

CHOICE TULIPS FOR FORCING

Generations of bulb lovers have discovered that some tulips are a lot better for forcing than others. As a rule, avoid choosing any bulbs that are less than three inches long (larger is fine). Experts at the Netherlands Flower Bulb Information Center recommend the following tulips for forcing:

RED:
BING CROSBY
CAPRI
CASSINI
PROMINENCE
RUBY RED
TRANCE

PINK:
Blenda
Cantor
Christmas Marvel
Gander
Preludium

YELLOW:
Bellona
Golden Melody
Kareol
Monte Carlo

WHITE:
Hibernia
Pax
Snowstar

APRICOT:
Apricot Beauty

LAVENDER:
Attila
Prince Charles

RED AND WHITE:
Lucky Strike
Merry Widow
Mirjoran

RED AND YELLOW:
Abra
Golden Mirjoran
Kees Nelis
Thule

SHOWY FORCING BLENDS

Forcing fanatics never tire of blending different tulips for effect, but experienced tulipomaniacs recognize that a jumble of color for color's sake is ultimately less attractive than a color scheme. For example, a rich backdrop of APRICOT BEAUTY—with its deep yet subtle tonalities of rose, ivory, cream, and lilac—is a wonderful way to display contrasting spots of yellow, lavender, and bicolored tulips. Avoid, however, a backdrop of pure white varieties splashed with bright primary colors—the contrast is often too stark. Instead, let white rule monochromatically, or use an off-shade for broad contrast with bright colors.

Your color scheme can be even more effective if you combine it with differing proportions—large pottings, small pottings, tall and short tulips that complement and echo each other, colorwise. Even if your colors are well-chosen and varied, identical height and identical pot size make for a boring display.

"Before they came, the air was calm enough,
Coming and going, breath by breath, without any fuss.
Then the tulips filled it up like a loud noise."
—Sylvia Plath

PLANT
THE WHITE HOUSE
TULIP GARDEN

George Washington and Thomas Jefferson were tulip-fanciers, with large plantings at their estates, and this tradition of presidential tulipomania continues to the present day. In fact, the White House Rose Garden contains enough seasonal tulip plantings to qualify as a genuine tulip garden—and you can model your own tulip landscape after the White House plan.

Beginning in early April, the White House blooms with *T. fosteriana* PURISSIMA and RED EMPEROR, followed in mid-April by Darwin hybrids that include cherry red APELDOORN, yellow-red GUDOSHNIK, golden yellow GOLDEN OXFORD, red OXFORD, pure white IVORY FLORENDALE, and deep yellow PRESIDENT KENNEDY. Spanning late April into May, *T. greigii* BOKARA and ORIENTAL

SPLENDOR add orange-red and red-yellow, respectively, along with the gold-edged red of lily-flowering QUEEN OF SHEBA and WHITE TRIUMPHATOR.

Through May, the tulip garden peaks with a rich variety, including cottage tulips such as lemony yellow-red BOND STREET, IVORY GLORY, and yellow MRS. J. T. SCHEEPERS. Also blooming in May are such Darwin tulips as vermilion red FLORENCE NIGHTINGALE, white FLYING DUTCHMAN, salmon-pink QUEEN OF THE BARLIGONS, white GLACIER, dark violet ARISTOCRAT, creamy yellow GOLDEN NIPHETOS, and the remarkable white-and-black ZWANENBURG. Parrot tulips BLACK PARROT and BLUE PARROT, pinkish-green FANTASY, and flaming ORANGE FAVORITE round out this Presidential tulip paradise!

RESOURCES

Tulip mail-order catalogs for purchasing the varieties named in this book are available from many sources, including the following:

Breck's
U.S. Reservation Center
6523 N. Galena Rd.
Peoria, IL 61632

Cruickshank's
1015 Mt. Pleasant Rd.
Toronto, ON
Canada M4P 2M1

Daffodil Mart
Rte. 3, Box 794
Gloucester, VA 23061
(804) 693-3966

Dutch Gardens
P.O. Box 200
Adelphia, NJ 07710
(908) 780-2713

John Scheepers Inc.
P.O. Box 700
Bantam, CT 06705
(203) 567-0838

K. Van Bourgondien and Sons Inc.
245 Farmingdale Rd.
P.O. Box 1000
Babylon, NY 11702-0598
(800) 552-9996

McClure & Zimmerman
P.O. Box 368
108 W. Winnebago
Friesland, WI 53935
(414) 326-4220

Peter de Jager Bulb Co.
188 Asbury St.
P.O. Box 2010
South Hamilton, MA 01982
(508) 468-4707

Van Dyck's Flower Farms
P.O. Box 430
Brightwaters, NY 11718-0430
(800) 248-2652

Van Engelen Inc.
Stillbrook Farm
313 Maple St.
Litchfield, CT 06759
(860)567-8734

"Here tulips bloom as they are told."
—RUPERT BROOKE

Recommended Tulip Tools

BULB AUGER

This clever invention lets you drill to the required depth for planting bulbs, and comes in varying widths, so choose according to the size of the bulbs you'll be planting. Some augers also attach to power drills, to make things even easier.

BULB PLANTER

They come in long, short, pricey, and cheap varieties, but buy the best—look for forged steel blades—and it'll last a long time while providing an efficient means of punching a perfect planting hole in the ground with minimal effort.

DIBBLE
A simple tool for making a hole to the required depth, the dibble, because of its pointed torpedo shape, is good for digging in hard-to-reach spots, near walls, etc.

GARDEN FORK
The wide area and sharp sod-cutting quality of this tool make it a good choice for opening up larger planting areas for placing quantities of bulbs in the ground.

TROWEL
If you have no other garden tool, or don't care to invest in the aforementioned ones, a trowel should get your bulbs planted quite nicely. Tulip bulbs tend to be large, and the large swathe of this classic gardener's hand shovel is appropriate for digging holes, in most cases.

Garden tools are widely available; some good mail-order sources are:

de Van Koek
9400 Business Dr.
Austin, TX 78758
(800) 992-1220

Gardener's Supply
128 Intervale Rd.
Burlington, VT 05401
(802) 863-1700

Langenbach
P.O. Box 453
Blairstown, NJ 07825
(800) 362-1991

Smith & Hawken
25 Corte Madera
Mill Valley, CA 94941-1829
(415) 383-2000